the children's
picture
dictionary

Text by Brenda Apsley

Illustrations by Jane Cunningham

World

a A

above

The bird is **above** the cat.

The cat is **above** the dog.

add

Add 2 and 3. The answer is 5.

against

The ladder leans **against** the wall.

The bike leans **against** the fence.

accident

David did not mean to break the jug.

It was an **accident.**

address

JOHN SMITH
10 HIGH ST
CHEADLE
CHESHIRE
SK8 1AL

Where you live is your **address.**

air

Air is all around us.

We breathe **air.**

We blow **air** into balloons.

acorn

An **acorn** is the fruit of the oak tree.

aeroplane

An **aeroplane** is a machine that flies.

airport

Aeroplanes land and take off at the **airport.**

across

The children walk **across** the crossing.

Passengers catch aeroplanes from the **airport.**

alike

The twins look the same.
They are **alike**.

The dogs are very different.
They are not **alike**.

alphabet

a b c d
e f g h
i j k l
m n o p
q r s t u
v w x y z

The letters of the **alphabet** make words.
There are 26 letters in the **alphabet**.

animal

Animals come in all shapes, sizes and colours.
A fish is an **animal**.
A cow is an **animal**.

mouse

elephant

lion

bear

horse

frog

snake

spider

parrot

giraffe

bat

all

All the flowers are red.

always

Always means every time, at all times.
Coal is **always** black.
Snow is **always** white.

alone

Susan is on her own.
She is **alone**.

and

And is a joining word.
Eggs **and** bacon.
Knife **and** fork.
Cup **and** saucer.

octopus

pig

along

The cat walks **along** the wall.
So does David.

angry

Susan is **angry**.

Here are more **angry** words: cross, furious.

Anything that lives and is not a plant is an **animal**.

ankle

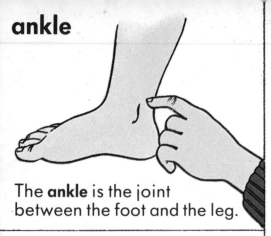

The **ankle** is the joint between the foot and the leg.

answer

The teacher asks a question.

David knows the **answer.**

Dad hurries to **answer** the telephone.

ant

An **ant** is a small insect.

apple

An **apple** is a fruit.

Apples grow on trees.

arm

The boy has two **arms.**

So does the chair.

So does the monkey.

arrow

An **arrow** is a pointed stick shot from a bow.

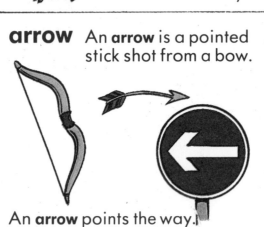

An **arrow** points the way.

artist

An **artist** is a person who paints or draws.

ask

WHAT TIME IS IT?

David **asks** a question.

asleep

The baby is not awake. The baby is **asleep.**

astronaut

An **astronaut** travels through space in a spaceship.

aunt

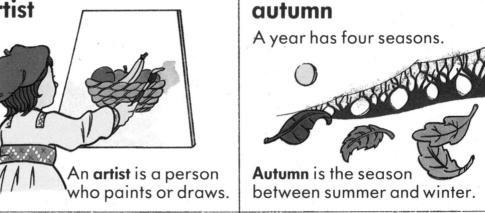

Daddy's sister is my **aunt.** Mummy's sister is my **aunt.**

autumn

A year has four seasons.

Autumn is the season between summer and winter.

awake

The baby is not asleep. The baby is **awake.**

b B

baby

A **baby** is a very young child.

bake

To **bake** is to cook in the oven.
Mum has **baked** a cake.

bank

A **bank** is a place to keep money in.

back

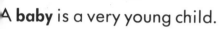

The children are standing back to **back**.

Susan takes her book back to the library.

ball

We play games with round **balls**.
The boy throws the **ball**.

bat

We play games with **bats**.

The boy will hit the ball with his **bat**.

balloon

Blow into the **balloon** to fill it with air.

beach

The **beach** is the sandy area by the sea.

bad

Sam is a **bad** dog.

Anything not good is **bad**.
The apple is **bad**.

band

A **band** is people who play music together.

beak

Birds eat with their **beaks.**

bed

We sleep in a **bed.**
Spot has his own **bed.**

bee

A **bee** is a black and yellow flying insect.
Bees make honey.

bell

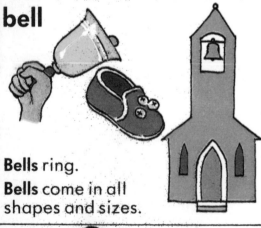

Bells ring.
Bells come in all shapes and sizes.

belt

Ben and Bob both
have brown belts.

between

Daddy is sitting
between the children.
Between means in the middle of.

bicycle

A **bicycle** has two wheels.
Can you ride a **bicycle**?

big

Big means large.
The red truck is **big.**

bigger

The blue truck is **bigger.**

biggest

The yellow truck is the biggest.

bird

A **bird** is an animal
with wings and feathers.
Most **birds** can fly.

sparrow

robin

pigeon

duck

penguin

turkey

toucan

ostrich

owl

hummingbird

eagle

peacock

gull

birthday

Today is John's fifth **birthday**.
He was born five years ago.

blanket

A **blanket** is a warm cover.
This **blanket** is blue.

book

Books have words and pictures.
Do you like reading **books**?

biscuit

Biscuits are sweet things to eat.

blow

The wind **blows**.
John **blows** his horn.

both

Both the girls have umbrellas.
Both the umbrellas have spots.

bite

The boy **bites** into his apple.

blue

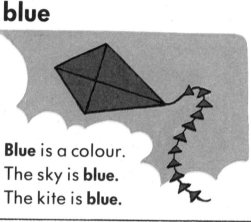

Blue is a colour.
The sky is **blue**.
The kite is **blue**.

bottom

Jack is at the **bottom** of the hill.
Jill is at the top.

black

The coal is **black**.
The cat is **black**.

boat

We ride on water in a **boat**.

Boats come in all shapes and sizes.

box

This **box** holds breakfast cereal.

This **box** holds chocolates.
What other things come in **boxes**?

blackboard

The teacher writes on the **blackboard**.

bread

Bread is good to eat.
The baker bakes **bread**.

breakfast

Breakfast is the meal we eat in the morning.
Susan is having a boiled egg for **breakfast**.

bubble

A **bubble** is round and filled with air.
Bubbles burst when you touch them.

James is blowing **bubbles**.

busy

Busy people have lots to do.

brick

Bricks are hard.
Many buildings are made of **brick**.

build

Build means to make something.
The **builder builds** a house.

Buildings come in all shapes and sizes.

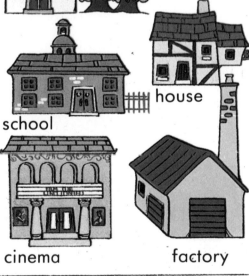

church

skyscraper

school

house

cinema

factory

butter

Butter is a food.
Butter tastes good on bread.

bridge

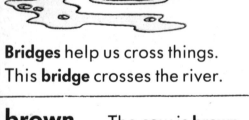

Bridges help us cross things.
This **bridge** crosses the river.

butterfly

A **butterfly** is an insect with four wings.

brown

The cow is **brown.**

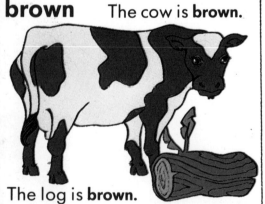

The log is **brown.**

button

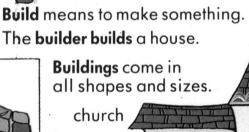

Buttons fasten John's coat.
The **buttons** are blue.

brush

Susan **brushes** her hair.

David **brushes** his teeth with a tooth **brush.**

bus

A **bus** carries many people. It is like a large car.

Do you go to school on a **bus**?

buy

Bob **buys** a boat.

Buy means to get something by paying money for it.

c C

cage

The hamster lives in a **cage**. The canary lives in a **cage**, too.

can

I **can** ride a bike.
I am able to ride a bike.

Cans hold things.

carpet

The **carpet** covers the floor.

cake

Susan has baked a **cake**.
Cakes are good to eat.

candle

A **candle** burns to give light.

Mary is putting **candles** on the cake.

carry

When you **carry** something you take it from one place to another.

Tim **carries** his case and book.

calendar

A **calendar** is a list of all the days and dates and months in a year.

What date does the **calendar** show?

car

A **car** is a machine that moves.
A **car** takes us from place to place.

castle

Castles were built long ago. They had many rooms, and thick walls to keep out the enemy.

camera

A **camera** is a machine that takes photographs.

careful

Be **careful** when you cross the road.

This **castle** is made of sand.

cat

A **cat** is a small, furry animal.
This **cat** is chasing leaves.

catch

The cat is trying to
catch the leaves.

The gardener is trying to
catch the cat.

caterpillar

A **caterpillar** is a grub which
turns into a butterfly or moth.

chair

We sit on **chairs.**

cheese

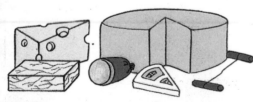

Cheese is a food made from milk.
There are many different
kinds of **cheese.**

chest

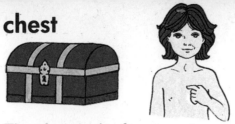

The **chest** is the front part
of the body between the neck
and the waist.
This is another kind of **chest** —
a toy **chest**, or box.

child

A **child** is a young boy or girl.

Christmas

Christmas is the
birthday of Jesus.

Christmas comes every
year on December 25th.

Let's decorate the
Christmas tree.

church

A **church** is a place
where people go to pray.

circle

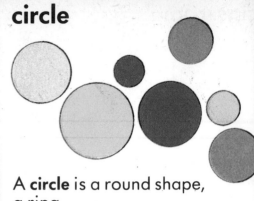

A **circle** is a round shape,
a ring.

circus

A **circus** is a special show.

acrobats

animals

clowns

city

A **city** is a ver
large tow

Many people live and work
in a **city**.

classroom

A **classroom** is a room in a school where children learn.

cloud

Clouds in the sky are white in good weather.

Clouds are dark in bad weather.

clean

Tom's face is **clean**. He's just washed it.

Tim's face isn't **clean**. It's dirty.

clothes

Clothes are things to wear.

pyjamas

dress

jacket

shirt

gloves

skirt

scarf

trousers

jumper

t-shirt

clown

Clowns have funny faces.

Clowns make us laugh.

climb

The child is **climbing** the stairs.

Plants **climb**, too.

coal

We burn **coal** for heat.

Coal is dug out of the ground.

coat

A **coat** keeps us warm.

Sheep have **coats**, too. Their woolly **coat** is called a fleece.

clock

A **clock** shows us what time it is.

Clocks come in all shapes and sizes.

cobweb

A **cobweb** is a fine net made by a spider to catch insects in.

coffee

Coffee is a drink.

Do you like **coffee**?

comb

A **comb** is used for tidying hair.
We **comb** our hair.

crawl

The boy **crawls** under the table.

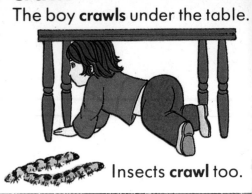

Insects **crawl** too.

cold

Cold is not hot.

Ice is **cold**.

Snow is **cold**.

Jane has a **cold**.
She is coughing and sneezing.

cook

Mummy makes lunch.
She **cooks** it.

This man
is a **cook**.

count

David is **counting** his money.
He is finding out how
much he has.

Can you **count**?

1 2 3 4 5 6 7 8 9 10

Count from 1 to 10.

cry

When James hurt his knee
he started to **cry**.

A **cry** is a loud shout, too.

cup

We drink from a **cup**.

The team won a silver **cup**.

curtain

Curtains cover the window.
Curtains keep out light.

colours

Everything has a **colour**.

The **colour** of the flower is pink.

The **colour** of the grass is green.

What **colour** is the ball?

cover

To **cover** means to put one
thing over another.
The blanket **covers**
the baby.

The book has a blue **cover**.

cut

Jane **cut** out a
paper doll.

Jane **cut** her finger
on the scissors.

d D

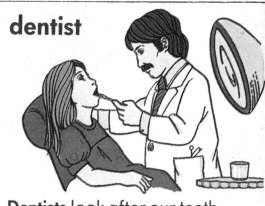

dance

Lucy is learning to **dance**.

day

A **day** is the time from morning till night.

It is light during the **day**.

dentist

Dentists look after our teeth.

danger

A **danger** sign means 'look out' or 'be careful'.

decide

Tim can't **decide** which t-shirt to have.

He can't make up his mind.

Susan can't **decide** which cake to choose.

She can't make up her mind.

describe

To **describe** means to tell more about.

Can you **describe** the dress?
The dress is blue.
The dress has short sleeves.
The dress has a pink belt.
The dress has two pockets.
The dress has a white collar.

dark

It is **dark** at night.

Dark means without light.

date

The **date** is what day, month and year it is.

A **date** is a sweet fruit.

deep

The cave is **deep**.

The sea is **deep**, but the pool is not **deep**.

Deep means how far in or down something goes.

desert

A **desert** is a large, dry, sandy area.

People ride camels in the **desert**.

desk

A **desk** is a table where we read, write and draw.

dig

Daddy **digs** in the garden. He turns the soil over.

dog

A **dog** is an animal with four legs.

Dogs are often kept as pets.

boxer

bulldog

dachshund

spaniel

greyhound

Great Dane

poodle

Some **dogs** work.

husky

sheepdog

dictionary

A **dictionary** is a book that lists words and what they mean. This book is a **dictionary**.

dirty

Daniel is digging too.

He is very **dirty**. He is not clean.

different

Different means not the same.

The ducks are **different**. They are not the same.

The cars are all **different**. They are not the same.

How many **different** toys do you have?

dive

The boy is going to **dive** into the water.

divide

To **divide** means to split into parts, or to share.

Mummy **divides** the pie into three pieces.

difficult

Difficult means not easy. **Difficult** means hard.

David thinks the sum is **difficult**. It is hard to do.

doctor

A **doctor** helps make sick people well.

These people are waiting to see the **doctor**.

doll

A **doll** is a toy.

These **dolls** are in a **dolls'** house.

draw

Dennis likes to **draw**.
What has Dennis **drawn**?

drive

The man **drives** a bus.

The woman **drives** a car.

donkey

A **donkey** looks like a small horse with big ears.

drawer

A **drawer** is a place to keep things in.

How many **drawers** does this chest have?

drop

A **drop** is a small amount of liquid.

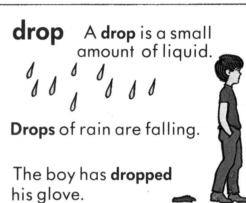

Drops of rain are falling.

The boy has **dropped** his glove.
He has let it fall.

door

We go in and out through **doors**.

One **door** is open, but the other **door** is closed.

dream

A **dream** is the pictures and thoughts in our minds as we sleep.

James **dreamed** he met a pink elephant.

David **dreamed** he was a king.

In Lucy's **dream** she was as small as a mouse.

drum

A **drum** is a musical instrument.
We beat the **drum** with sticks.

down

James is walking **down** the street.

dry

The wind will blow the washing **dry**.

David's hands are wet.

He **dries** them with a towel.

downstairs

James is walking **down** the stairs.
He is going **downstairs**.

drink

Can I have a **drink** of milk, please?

dust

Dust is very tiny bits of dirt.

Diana **dusts** the furniture.
She uses a **duster**.

e E

ear

The **ear** is what we hear sound with.

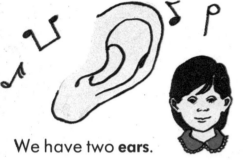

We have two **ears**.

easy

Easy means not hard, not difficult.

The jigsaw puzzle is **easy** to do. It's simple.

egg

Baby birds are born from **eggs**. We eat chicken and duck **eggs**.

We eat chocolate Easter **eggs**, too.

early

The train is **early**. It is ahead of time.

Try to be **early**. Try not to be late

eat

Eat means to bite, chew and swallow food.

The children are **eating** hamburgers.

eight

Eight tells us how many.

Eight eggs.

1   2 3 4 5 6 7 8

earth

Our world is called the **earth**. We live on the planet **earth**.

Earth is soil.

Flowers, trees and plants grow in **earth**.

echo

An **echo** is a sound which bounces back.

Listen for the **echo** of your voice in a cave, tunnel or empty building.

edge

The knife blade has a sharp **edge**.

The vase is on the **edge** of the table.

elbow

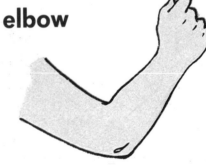

The **elbow** is the part of the arm that bends.

electricity

Electricity is the power used to make light and heat

Electricity drives machines, too

elephant

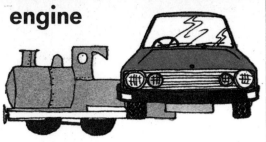

The **elephant** is the largest four-footed animal in the world.
Elephants have long trunks.

engine

An **engine** is a machine.
The **engine** in a car makes it go.
The **engine** pulls the train.

evening

Evening is the last part of the day.
After **evening** comes night.

eleven

Eleven tells us how many.

Eleven elephants.

enormous

Enormous means very large.
Eric is eating an **enormous** icecream.

enough

Enough means as much as is needed.
Jane has **enough** money to buy the teddy.

every

We wake up **every** morning.

We wash **every** morning.

We eat breakfast **every** morning.

empty

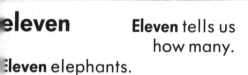

Jane's purse is **empty**.
There is nothing in it.

envelope

We put letters in **envelopes** before posting them.

exit

Exit means way out.

end

Jim is at one **end** of the rope.

John is at the other **end**.

end also means to stop or finish.

escalator

An **escalator** is a moving stairway.

eye

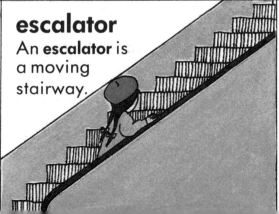

The **eye** is the part of the body used for seeing.
We see with our **eyes**.

f F

face

The **face** is the front part of the head.

The eyes, nose and mouth are part of the **face**.

fall

In autumn the leaves **fall** from the trees.

fasten

Fasten means to join together or lock.

Daddy **fastens** his seat belt.

fact

A **fact** is something that is true.

It is a **fact** that Bob has black hair.

family

Mummy, Daddy and the children are a **family**.

Aunts, uncles and cousins are part of the **family**, too.

fat

All the pigs are **fat**. They are large and round.

One pig is **fatter** than the others.

factory

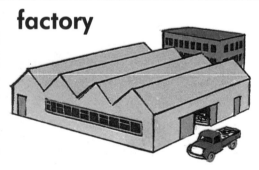

A **factory** is a place where things are made.

farm

A **farm** is a place where crops are grown, and animals are kept.

feel

Feel the cat's fur. Does it **feel** silky?

fail

To **fail** is to be unable to do something.

The dog **failed** to catch the cat.

farmer

The **farmer** looks after the farm.

fence

The **fence** keeps the cows in the field.

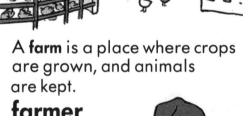

Does your garden have a **fence**

few

Few means not many.
Fred only has a few marbles.

finger

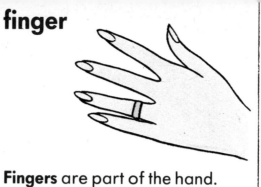

Fingers are part of the hand.
Which finger has a ring on it?

fish A fish is an animal that lives in water.

cod

eel

goldfish

salmon

seahorse

plaice

swordfish

shark

field

A field is a piece of land.
Corn is growing in the field.

finish

Daddy finished the story.
He read it to the end.

fight

The children are fighting.
They both want the ball.

fire A fire burns.
We put coal on the fire.

Fires can be dangerous.

The fire engine
carries the firemen.
The fireman helps
to put out fires.

fit

The shoe is
a good fit.

It's not too big
and not too small.

fill David has filled his glass
with milk.

There is no room for any more.
The glass is full.

find

Susan is trying to find her doll.
Can you see it?

first

The boy won the race.
He came first.

five Five tells us how many.

1 2 3 4 5

Five foxes.

flag

Every country has its own **flag**.
The **flag** is the sign
of the country.

flat

The table top is **flat**.
It is smooth and level.

The boys live in a **flat**.
All the rooms are on one floor.

float

The boat **floats** on the water.
It stays on top of the water.

flock

A group of sheep is a **flock**.

floor

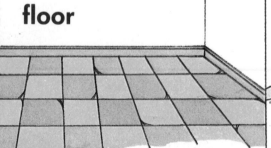

The **floor** is the part of
a room we walk on.

flower

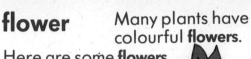

Many plants have
colourful **flowers**.
Here are some **flowers**.

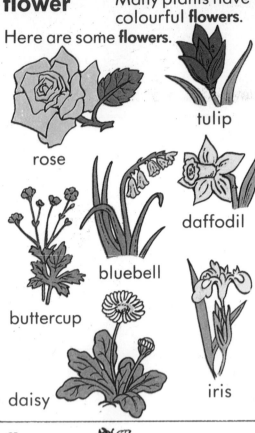

rose

tulip

daffodil

bluebell

buttercup

daisy

iris

fly

A **fly** is a small insect with wings.
It **flies** through the air.

Aeroplanes **fly**.
So do most birds.

fog

Fog is very thick mist.

It is hard to see
in **foggy** weather.

follow

The little boy **follows**
his brother.
He walks behind him.

food

Food is all the things we eat.

bread

cheese

carrots

chicken

milk

icecream

potatoes

nuts

biscuits

spaghetti

pear

foot

The **foot** is at the
end of the leg.

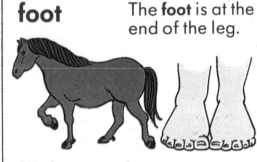

We have two **feet**.
The horse has four **feet**.

forest

A **forest** is a large
group of trees.

forget

Don't **forget** to take your books to school.

Don't leave them behind.

four

Four tells us how many.

1
2
3
4

Four frogs.

free

It doesn't cost anything to get into the park.

It is **free**.

freeze

When something **freezes** it turns to ice.

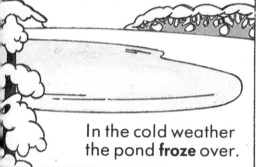

In the cold weather the pond **froze** over.

friend

The children like each other. They are **friends**.

front

Fred is at the **front** of the queue.

Fred's name is on the **front** of his t-shirt.

fruit

A **fruit** is the part of a plant or tree that holds the seeds.

The apple is the **fruit** of the apple tree.

banana

blackberries

cherries

grapefruit

lemon

orange

melon

gooseberries

plum

fig

apricot

peach

funny

The clown is **funny**.

The clown makes the boy laugh. Do you know any **funny** jokes?

fur

The soft hairs on an animal's body are its **fur**.

The polar bear has white **fur**. The bear has brown **fur**.

furniture

Things in the rooms of a house are called **furniture**.

All these things are **furniture**.

bed

dressing table

wardrobe

table

chest of drawers

chair

stool

sofa

desk

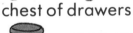

bookcase

lamp

g G

game

We play many **games**.

football

golf

marbles

cards

hide and seek

chess

dominoes

noughts and crosses

Games are fun.

gift

A **gift** is a present.

David has brought Susan a **gift** for her birthday.

giraffe

The **giraffe** is the tallest animal in the world.

garage

A **garage** is a place where cars are kept.

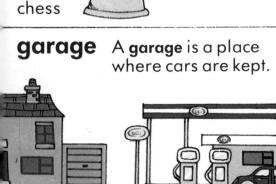

Large **garages** sell petrol and repair cars.

gate

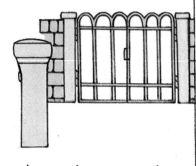

A **gate** is an opening in a fence or wall.

glass

Glass is hard and clear. We can usually see through it.

Glasses help us see better.

garden

A **garden** is a piece of ground for growing things in.

get

How much pocket money do you **get**?

glove

Gloves are worn on the hands.

Gloves keep hands warm and d

goat

A **goat** is an animal with horns and a beard.

Goat milk is good to drink.

gorilla

The **gorilla** is the largest, strongest ape.

Gorillas live in Africa.

group

A **group** is a number of things.

A **group** of people.
A **group** of pictures.

gold

Gold is a yellow metal.

All these things are made of **gold**.

grandparents

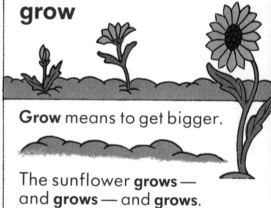

Mummy and Daddy's parents are our **grandparents**.

grow

Grow means to get bigger.

The sunflower **grows** — and **grows** — and **grows**.

goldfish

Goldfish are gold coloured.

Goldfish are good pets.

grape

A **grape** is a small fruit.

Grapes grow in bunches.

growl

A **growl** is an angry sound made by a lion.

Dogs **growl**, too.

goodbye

Father is going away.

He waves **goodbye**.

grass

Grass is a plant with long, thin leaves.

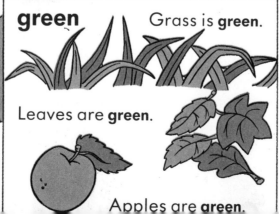

guess

If we **guess** we are not really sure.

Can you **guess** what is in the parcel?

goose

A **goose** is a large bird with webbed feet and a long neck.
Geese are good swimmers.

green

Grass is **green**.

Leaves are **green**.

Apples are **green**.

guitar

A **guitar** is a musical instrument with strings.

h H

hair
Hair grows on your head.

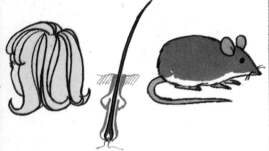

Animals have **hair**, too.

handle
A **handle** is something to hold.

The pan, the mug and the door all have **handles**.

hat
You wear a **hat** on your head.

Which **hat** do you like best?

half
The orange has been cut in **half**.

The two **halves** are exactly the same.

happy

When we are **happy** we are very pleased.

head

The **head** is the part of the body above the neck.

Head also means front or top. Hugh is at the **head** of the queue

hand
You have two **hands**.

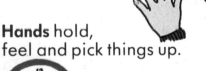

Hands hold, feel and pick things up.

Clocks have **hands**, too.

hard
Hard means solid, firm.
Hard means not soft.

Which of these things are **hard**?

Riding the bicycle is **hard**. It is not easy.

hear
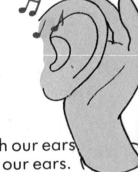

We listen with our ears. We **hear** with our ears. What can you **hear** now?

handkerchief

A **handkerchief** is a piece of cloth for wiping the nose. Hankie is another name for **handkerchief**.

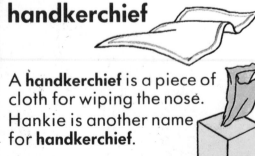

Soft paper **handkerchieves** are called tissues.

heart

The **heart** pumps blood through our bodies.

Can you hear your **heart** beating?

heavy

Henry can't lift the suitcase.

It is too **heavy**.

hen

A **hen** is a bird that lays eggs.

hole

The doughnut has a **hole** in it.

The sock has a **hole**, too.

heel

The **heel** is the back part of the foot.

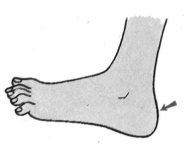

hide

The kitten is **hiding** under the table.

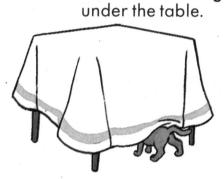

holiday

A **holiday** is a day when there is no work, no school. Christmas is a **holiday**.

Where do you go for your summer **holidays**?

helicopter

A **helicopter** is a machine that flies.

Instead of wings it has whirring blades.

hello

Hello is a greeting. **Hello** is a friendly word.

help

Helen is **helping** Mummy to wash the dishes.

To **help** is to do something for someone.

high

High means far up.

The sun is **high** in the sky.

The building is **high**.

How **high** can you jump?

hill

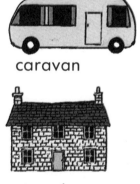

A **hill** is a high piece of ground. How many **hills** can you see?

home

A **home** is a place to live. Where is your **home**?

flats

houseboat

caravan

igloo

stone house

grass hut

Animals have **homes**, too.

kennel

nest

burrow

hop

Mary can jump on one leg.
She can **hop**.

hospital

A **hospital** is a place where
people go when they are ill.

how

How means in what way
Harry is learning **how**
to play the piano.

How means what amount.
How old are you?

How means in what condition.
How are you feeling today?

horn

Some animals have **horns**.
Horns are hard.

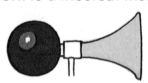

A **horn** is a musical instrument.

A car **horn** makes
a warning sound.

hot

The soup is too warm to drink.
It's too **hot**.

hotel

A **hotel** is a building where
people eat and sleep when
they are away from home.

hungry

Spot is **hungry**.
He wants some food.

horse

A **horse** is a four-footed animal.
Some **horses** run races.

Some **horses** pull carts.

Many people ride **horses**.

hour

An **hour** is a measure of time.

There is an **hour** between
two o'clock and three o'clock.

house

A **house** is a building we live in.

hurry

When we
hurry
we do something quickly.

hurt

The boy has **hurt** his arm.
He has injured it.

i l

ice

Ice is frozen water.

Ice keeps food cold.

ill

Tom is ill. He is not well.

inside

The **inside** of the box is red. The outside is blue.

What is **inside** the box?

icecream

Icecream is good to eat.
Icecream is cold.

ink

Ink is coloured liquid.

We fill pens with **ink** to write with.

invite

To **invite** is to ask to come.

Who are you going to **invite** to your party?

I'm going to **invite** the whole class!

icicle

When it is very cold, running water may freeze and make **icicles**.

insect

An **insect** is a small animal with six legs.

flea

ladybird

bee

dragonfly

beetle

moth

stick insect

iron

Mummy uses an **iron** to **iron** my dress.

It makes it smooth and flat.
Iron is a hard metal.

idea

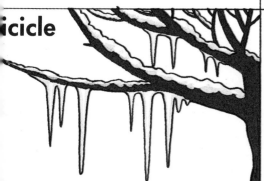

An **idea** is a thought or plan.

What shall we play? Any **ideas**?

I've got a great **idea** — let's play hide and seek!

island

An **island** is a piece of land with water all around it.

j J

jacket

A **jacket** is a short coat.

job

A **job** is something that people work at.

Teaching is a **job**.

Driving is a **job**.

jug

A **jug** holds things

juice

What is in the jug? Orange **juice**!

jam

Jam is a sweet food made of fruit and sugar.

jar

The jam is in a glass **jar**.

joke

A **joke** makes people laugh.

Paul is going to play a **joke**.

jump

Jane **jumps** over the rope

jeans

Jeans are kinds of trousers.

journey

These people are going on a trip. They are going on a **journey**.

jungle

Can you see any wild animals in the **jungle**?

jelly

A **jelly** is a cold, clear, fruity pudding.

A **jellyfish** is a water animal.

judge

Mrs Smith is **judging** the onions. She's deciding which are best.

just

It is **just** two o'clock. It is exactly two o'clock

k K

keep
Where do you **keep** your bike?

In the shed.

kiss

Karen gives her doll a **kiss**.

knee

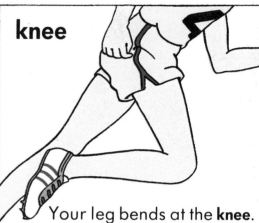

Your leg bends at the **knee**.

key

Keys open and shut locks.

kitchen
The **kitchen** is the room where food is cooked.

knife
A **knife** is used for cutting.

kick

evin **kicks** the football.

kite

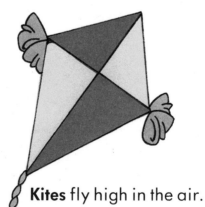

Kites fly high in the air.

knock
Keith **knocks** at the door.

Keith has **knocked** over the milk bottle.

ind
he boy is **kind** to his rabbit. e treats it well.

What **kind** of rabbit is it? What sort of rabbit is it?

kitten
A **kitten** is a young cat.

This **kitten** is trying to catch the kite.

knot

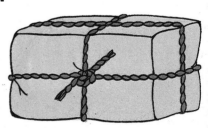

A **knot** ties things together. There is a **knot** in the string.

l L

ladder

A **ladder** is a set of steps that can be moved around.

lazy

A **lazy** person is one who does not want to work.

left

Lenny holds up his **left** foo

Linda holds up her **left** hand.

lamb

A **lamb** is a young sheep.

lead

The drummer **leads** the band. The drummer is at the front.

letter

There are 26 **letters** in the alphabet.

The postman puts a **letter** in the **letterbox**.

A **letter** is a message.

large

Large means big.

Pick out the **large** leaf.

leaf

Leaves grow on trees, plants and bushes.

Leaves are usually green.

library

A **library** is a place where books are kep

Do you borrow books from a **library**?

late

Laurence is **late** for school.

He is not on time.

leave

Shall I move the chair? No, **leave** it there.

I'm going to **leave** now. I'm going away.

lid

The pan's cover is called a **lid**.

Eyes have **lids**, too

lie To **lie** means to rest flat.
The boy **lies** on the bed.

Lie also means to say
something that isn't true.

like To **like** means to enjoy
or be pleased by.

Do you **like** icecream?

Do you **like** to play?

lock

When things are **locked**, they
cannot be opened without a key.
The door has a **lock**.

So does the box.

lift The man **lifts** the box.

He moves it higher.

Lifts are machines that
move people up or down.

Tall buildings have **lifts**
instead of stairs.

line The children form a **line**.
They make a row.

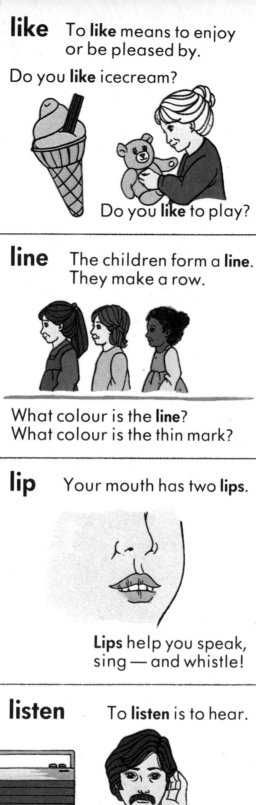

What colour is the **line**?
What colour is the thin mark?

lip Your mouth has two **lips**.

Lips help you speak,
sing — and whistle!

look

Leo **looks** at the
bird.
Lynn **looks**, too.

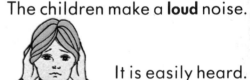

Larry **looks** in a mirror.

loud

The children make a **loud** noise.

It is easily heard.

light These things are **light**.

They are not heavy.
They are easy to pick up.

It is **light** during the day.
The electric bulb makes **light**.

One pair of jeans are dark blue.
The other pair are **light** blue.

listen To **listen** is to hear.

The man is **listening** to music.

loaf A **loaf** is a piece of bread.

Can you see a brown **loaf**?

low

The bush is **low**.
It is near the
ground.

Is the tree **low**?

lunch

Lunch is a meal eaten
in the middle of the day.

m M

machine

A **machine** helps us to get work done.

Machines make jobs easier.

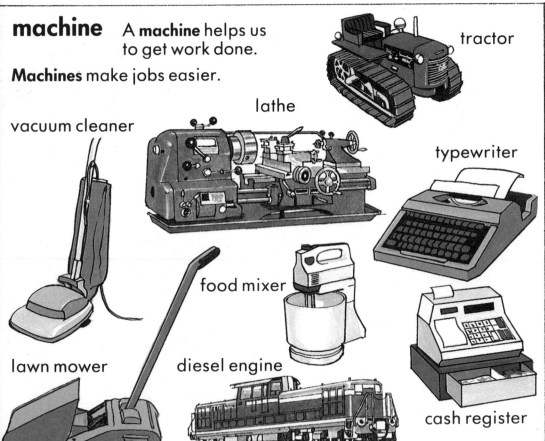

tractor

lathe

vacuum cleaner

typewriter

food mixer

lawn mower

diesel engine

cash register

map

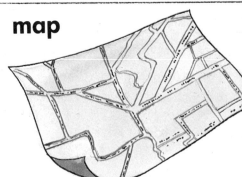

A **map** helps us find our way.
A **map** shows us where things a

march

When we **march** we walk in line
When we **march** we keep in step

magic

The man pulled scarves from a hat.

It was a trick. It was **magic**.

man

When he grows up the boy will be a **man**.

mark

There is a dirty **mark** on Susan's dress.

The teacher **marks** David's sum
She **marks** which are right —
and which are wrong.

make

Matt **makes** a castle.

Matt **makes** a cake

many

There are **many** people watching football.

There are a lot of people.

How **many**?

The line **marks** where the race starts.
On your **mark**, get set, GO!

market

A **market** is a busy place where things are bought and sold.

meet

The ladies **meet** at the market every week. They go to see each other.

mirror

You can see yourself in a **mirror**. **Mirrors** are made of glass.

mat

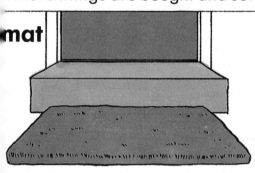

A **mat** is a small rug.

melt When ice and snow **melt** they change to water.

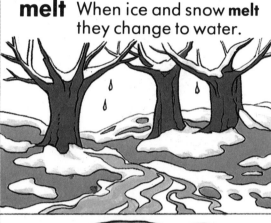

miss

David **missed** the target. He failed to hit the target.

match

Mary's hat, gloves and scarf **match**. They are all the same colour.

Mummy uses a **match** to light the fire.

Let's watch the tennis **match**. A **match** is a game, or contest.

middle

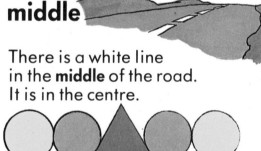

There is a white line in the **middle** of the road. It is in the centre.

The triangle is in the **middle** of the circles.

Susan **missed** the bus. It went without her.

milk

Milk comes from cows. **Milk** is good to drink.

mistake

Mike put salt in his tea. It was a **mistake**. He didn't mean to do it.

measure

To **measure** is to find the size or amount of something.

Mummy **measures** out some milk.

Daddy **measures** a piece of wood.

minute

A **minute** is a measure of time. There are 60 seconds in a **minute**. There are 60 **minutes** in an hour.

mix

To **mix** means to put together. Mummy **mixes** a cake **mix**.

money

Money is used to buy things.

Money is coins.

Money is banknotes.

moon

The **moon** shines in the night sky.

The **moon** changes shape.

more

Mark wants **more** pie.

He wants another piece.

mouth

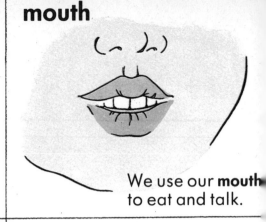

We use our **mouth** to eat and talk.

move

Move means to go to another place.

The train **moves** out of the station.
Move means to put somewhere else.

The dog **moves** his bone to a new hole.

monkey

A **monkey** is a tree-climbing animal.

morning

Morning is the first part of the day.

much

How **much** is it to New Road?
What does it cost?

month

A **month** is part of a year.
There are twelve **months** in a year.
Can you name them?

January	February	March
April	May	June
July	August	September
October	November	December

mountain

A **mountain** is a very high piece of land.

Which is higher — a **mountain** or a hill?

mouse

A **mouse** is a small furry animal with a long tail.

Mice make good pets.

music

Music is pleasing sounds made by instruments or voices.

musical instruments

violin

piano

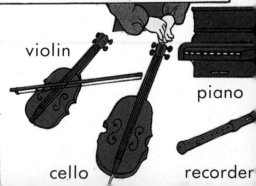

cello

recorder

n N

nail

Metal **nails** hold things together.

We have **nails** on our fingers and toes.

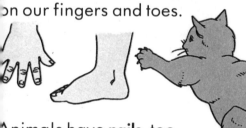

Animals have **nails,** too. They are called claws.

near

The dog sits **near** his owner. He sits close to his owner.

nearly

Number 5 **nearly** won the race. He almost won.

neighbour

Neighbours live near each other. The two boys are **neighbours.**

neither

Which bun would you like? **Neither**, I don't like buns.

Neither means not one or the other.

name

Our **name** is what we are called. Our **name** is what we are known as.

What is your **name**?

neck   Nancy's **neck** is short.

The giraffe's **neck** is long.

nest   A bird's home is a **nest**.

Ants live in **nests**, too.

narrow

The gap in the fence is **narrow**. It is not wide.

need

Need means must have.

Ned **needs** a bath.

never   Never means not ever.

Never cross the road without looking both ways.

new The blue car is **new**.

The green car isn't **new**.
It's very old.

night It is dark at **night**.

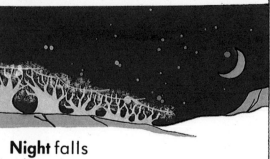

Night falls
when the sun goes down.

nose We breathe and smel
through our **noses**.

The dog smells
with his **nose**, too.

news

The **news** tells us
what has been happening.

nine **Nine** tells us how many.

Here are **nine nines**!

9	9	9
9	9	9
9	9	9

number

A **number** tells us how many.

Do you know the **numbers**
from 1 to 20?

1	2	3	4
5	6	7	8
9	10	11	12
13	14	15	16
17	18	19	20

newspaper

We read the news
in a **newspaper**.

nobody

Who is in the
classroom?

$4 \times 7 =$

Nobody! It's empty.

next

Next means nearest to.
The houses are **next** to each other.

a b c d

What is the **next** letter after d?
The **next** letter is e.

Next,
please!

noise **Noises** are sounds.

The dog's bark is a **noise**.

The car's horn makes a **noise**.

none **None** means not one.

None of the children
have blond hair.
Not one has blond hair

nurse

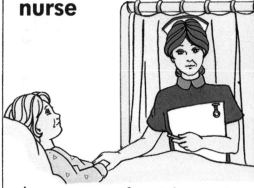

A **nurse** cares for sick people.

nut **Nuts** are the seeds of
some plants and trees.

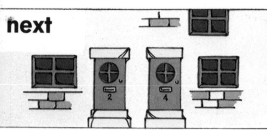

peanut

hazelnut

walnut

Nuts have hard shells.

o O

oak The **oak** is a large tree.

Its fruit is the acorn.

office

An **office** is where people work.

once

Once means at one time.

Dinosaurs **once** lived on earth.

ocean

An **ocean** is a large sea.

Do you know the names of any **oceans**?

oil Oil is liquid grease.

Daddy puts **oil** in his car engine. It helps it to run smoothly.

one One tells us how many.

Oliver has **one** white glove and **one** black.

odd Which is the **odd** sock?

Which sock is different from the rest?

Mummy uses cooking **oil**. She fries food in it.

only

Only one of the sweets is red.

off Off means not on.

David turned the radio **off**.

The ball rolled **off** the bed.

old The train is **old**. It is not new.

How **old** are you?

open The window is **open**.

The door is **open**.

They are not closed.

orange

An **orange** is a fruit.

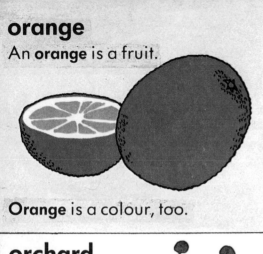

Orange is a colour, too.

other

I don't like this hat. Have you any **others**?

Have you any different ones?

over

Jane holds the umbrella **over** her head.

When will this programme be **over**? When will it finish?

How many nails are there? **Over** twenty. More than twenty.

orchard

An **orchard** is where fruit trees grow.

What is growing in this **orchard**? Oranges!

out

David and Susan look **out** of the window.

"Shall we go **out**?" says David.

order   An **order** is a command.

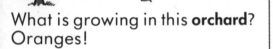

The officer shouts **orders**, and the soldiers obey.

a b c d e f g

The letters are in alphabetical **order**.

We don't have your size, but we can **order** it.

outdoors

David is going **outdoors**.

Susan is **outdoors** already.

overalls

Oliver wears **overalls** to paint. They cover him all over.

outside

David and Susan are **outside** the house.

They are not inside.

owl

An **owl** is a bird with large eyes

organ   **Organs** make music.

Organs are in most churches.

oven

What is baking in the **oven**?

It's a pie!

own

The girl has a puppy of her **own**. It belongs to her.

Say some things that you **own**

p P

page Books and newspapers have **pages**.

How many **pages** in this book?

pain Peter is in **pain**. His knee hurts.

palm The inside of your hand is called the **palm**.

A **palm** is a tall tree. It grows in warm lands.

parent

A **parent** is a father or mother. Mummy is a **parent**.

Daddy is a **parent**.

park

A **park** is an open space, with grass, trees and flowers.

Some **parks** have a playground, too.

paint Pat **paints** a picture.

Daddy **paints** the shed. What colour is the **paint**?

paper

We write and draw on **paper**.
We read from **paper**.
We hang **paper** on walls.
We wrap things in **paper**.

party

Friends have fun together at a **party**.

Whose **party** do you think it is?

pair A **pair** means two things that match.

Can you see a **pair** of mittens?

parcel A **parcel** is a small package.

What is the **parcel** wrapped in? Paper!

pavement

A **pavement** is a path beside the road, for people to walk on.

pay

I'll **pay** for your ticket.
I'll give the money for it.

pen

A **pen** writes with ink.

pencil

We write with **pencils**, too.

people

Human beings are **people**.

Men and women,
boys and girls are **people**.

pet

A **pet** is an animal that we feed and take care of.

goldfish

Do you have a **pet**?

mouse

dog

canary

rabbit

cat

hamster

picnic

At **picnics** we eat outdoors.

picture

A **picture** is a drawing, painting or photograph.

There are **pictures** on this page.

piece

The cake has been cut into **pieces**.

One **piece** is missing!

pile

Paula swept the leaves into a **pile**.

pin

Pins fasten things.

Can you name these **pins**?

plant

Trees, flowers, bushes and grasses are all **plants**.

Daddy is **planting** some bulbs.

He is putting them in the ground.

We are all **people**.

plate

We eat food from a **plate**.

pocket

What does Peter have in his **pocket**?

A puppy!

pull

The children **pull** hard on the rope. They draw it towards them.

play

A **play** is a show.

This is the school **play**.

The children **play** a game at **play**time.

Pete **plays** a guitar.

pond

A **pond** is a small pool of water.

pony

A **pony** is a small horse.

puppet

Puppets are dolls that move.

A hand moves one **puppet**. Strings move the other **puppet**.

push

Mummy **pushes** a pram.

playground

A **playground** is a special place to play.

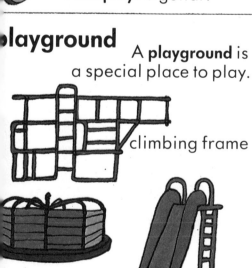

climbing frame

roundabout

slide

seesaw

swings

post

Pete **posts** a letter. He sends it. The **postman** delivers the letter.

Have you been to a **post office**?

prize

A **prize** is something you get for winning or doing well.

Paul's picture won a **prize**

put

David **puts** his sock on.

Daddy **puts** the teapot on the table.

puzzle

Pam is doing a jigsaw **puzzle**.

She doesn't know where the pieces go. She is **puzzled**.

q Q

quack

Quack is the noise a duck makes.

question

The teacher asks a **question**.

"What is today's date?"

The children answer her **question**.

quiet

Quiet, don't make a noise, the baby's sleeping.

quantity

Quantity is the amount or size of something.

Daddy ordered a large **quantity** of bricks.

queue

The children **queue** at the bus stop.

They stand in line, one behind the other.

quilt

A **quilt** is a warm, thick bed cover.

quarrel

The children both want the book.

They are angry.
They are **quarrelling**.

quite

Susan isn't **quite** as tall as Davi
She is nearly as tall.

quarter

To **quarter** is to cut into four equal parts.

A **quarter** is one of four equal parts.

quick

Quick means very fast.

Susan runs **quickly**.

quiz

A **quiz** is a test.

People doing a **quiz** have to answer questions.

r R

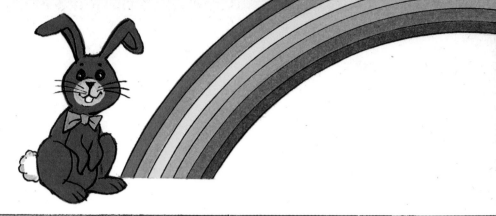

race

The fastest runner will win the **race**.

Cars and horses **race**, too.

reach

Roy cannot **reach** the lemonade. He cannot touch it.

rest

All the **rest** are blue.

One ball is green.
All the **rest** are blue.

All the others are blue.

rain

rain is drops of water which fall from the clouds.

Do you like **rainy** weather?

real

Which is the **real** rabbit?
Which is the toy rabbit?

rest

Robin is tired.
He **rests** on his bed.

rainbow

When sun shines through rain we see a **rainbow**.

A **rainbow** is a band of colour.

red

Red is a colour.

All these things are **red**.

riddle

A **riddle** is a word puzzle.
Here's a **riddle**.

What is black and white and read all over?

A newspaper!

raw

Raw means not cooked.

Which foods do we eat **raw**?

remember

Can you **remember** what you got for Christmas?

Can you think back?

ride

To **ride** is to go somewhere on something.
We **ride** on bicycles.

We **ride** on buses.

We **ride** on horses.

right

Tom holds up his **right** hand.
Hold up your **right** hand.

Tom got his sum **right**.
His sum is correct.

ring

Do you wear a **ring** on your finger?

The circus **ring** is round.

Roy **rings** the doorbell.

river

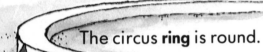 

A **river** is a large stream of water.

road

Cars and buses travel on **roads**.

We cross the **road** at crossings.

rock

Rock is stone.

Grandma **rocks**
in her rocking chair.

roll

A **roll** is a small piece of bread.

The man **rolls** up the carpet.

The marbles **roll** across the floor.
So does David!

roof

A **roof** covers the top of buildings.

room

Rooms are different
parts of the house.

This is David's **room**.

rough

The sea is **rough**. It is not smooth

How does an egg feel?
Smooth or **rough**?

round

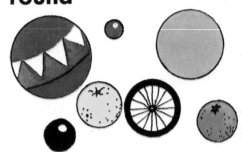

All these things are **round**

row

The flowers are planted in a **row**
They are in a line.

The man **rows** a **row**ing boat.
He uses wooden oars.

run   To **run** is to move quickl

The man and the dog **run** quickl
The stream **runs**, too.

s S

sack

sack A **sack** is a large bag.

The children are in a **sack** race.

scare

scare To **scare** means to frighten.

Sam is trying to **scare** his sister.
She doesn't look **scared**, does she?

sea

sea The **sea** is a very big area of salt water.

The **seaside** is beside the **sea**.

same

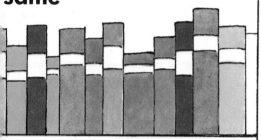

Which two books are the **same**?
Which two are alike?

sand

Sand is very tiny pieces of rock.

Sand is in the desert.

Sand is on the beach.

school

We go to **school** to learn.

Do you go to **school**?

season

There are four **seasons** in a year.

spring

summer

autumn

winter

save

save To **save** is to keep something.

Sue **saves** her money.
She is **saving** to buy a doll.

scissors

scissors **Scissors** are two sharp blades.

Scissors cut paper, cloth — and hair!

seat

seat A **seat** is something to sit on.

A chair is a **seat**.

So is a stool.

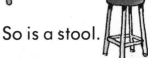

seed

Plants grow from **seeds**.
The tall sunflower grew from the tiny **seed**.

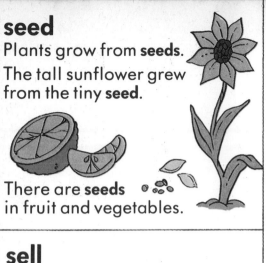

There are **seeds** in fruit and vegetables.

sell

To **sell** is to give things for money.

This shop **sells** fish.

sense

To **sense** means to feel.
We **sense** that the air is cold.

Our **senses** help us to see, hear, smell, taste and touch.

shape

Shape is the form things take.
Here are some different **shapes**.

round   square

rectangle

triangle

What **shape** is the sun?

sheep

A **sheep** is an animal.

A **sheep** has hair called wool.

We make clothes from the wool of **sheep**.

shell

A **shell** is an outside cover.

Animals have **shells**.

tortoise   snail

Nuts have **shells**.

Eggs have **shells**.

shoe

Shoes cover feet.
What do you wear under **shoes**?

Horses wear **shoes**, too — horse**shoes**.

shop

A **shop** is where we go to buy things.

What is sold in the blue **shop**?

Can you see the **shopkeeper**

shut

Shut means to close or fasten.

The door and the window are **shut**.
Is the cupboard **shut**?

sing

When we **sing**, we make music with our voices.
The children **sing**.

Birds **sing**, too.

seven

Seven tells us how many.

1 2 3 4 5
6 7

ship

A **ship** is a very large boat.

six

Six tells us how many.

How many soldiers? **Six!**

size

Size tells us how big or small things are.

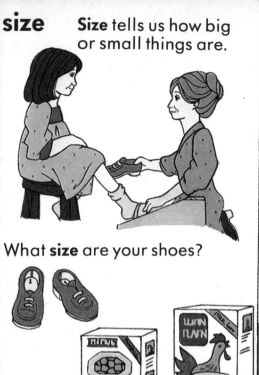

What **size** are your shoes?

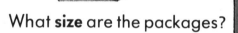

SMALL SIZE   LARGE SIZE

What **size** are the packages?

sleep

When we **sleep** we rest our body and mind.

The child is **sleeping**. He is **asleep**.

smile

We **smile** when we are happy.

snow

When rain freezes it turns to **snow**. **Snowflakes** fall from the air.

The children build a **snowman**. They throw **snowballs**.

soap

Soap helps us clean things.

We wash our bodies with **soap**. We wash clothes with **soap** powder.

skate

Can you **skate**?

One child wears ice **skates**. The other wears roller **skates**.

smoke

Smoke comes from fires.

soft

Soft means not hard, not loud.

David's pillow is **soft**.

Mummy speaks in a **soft** voice.

skin

Your body is covered in **skin**.

An apple is covered in **skin**, too.

smooth

Smooth means flat, without any bumps.

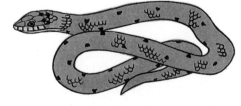

The paper is **smooth**.

sound

We hear **sounds**.

Sound is noise.

sky

The **sky** is the space above the earth.

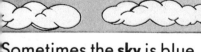

Sometimes the **sky** is blue.

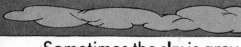

Sometimes the **sky** is grey. What colour is the **sky** today?

snake

A **snake** is a long thin animal.

Snakes have no legs. Do you think **snakes** are smooth?

speak

The teacher **speaks** to the class. She talks to them.

stairs

Stairs are steps.

We go up**stairs** and come down**stairs**.

stick

A **stick** is a small piece of wood.
Stan hit the stone with a **stick**.

We **stick** things together with glue.

street

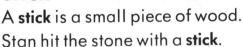

A **street** is a small road in a town or city.

stamp

A **stamp** shows you have paid to send a letter.

Some people collect **stamps** from different countries.

Sue is angry. She **stamps** her foot.

stop

Stop means to finish or halt.

The bus **stops** at a bus **stop**.

strong

The man is **strong**. He can lift heavy things.

star

We see **stars** in the sky at night.

Can you count all the **stars**?

Sarah draws a **star** shape.

storm

In a **storm** it rains hard and the wind blows.

In **stormy** weather we may see thunder and lightning, too.

sun

The **sun** warms the earth and gives it light.

Today is a **sunny** day. The people are **sunbathing** in the **sunshine**.

start

To **start** means to begin.

The runners wait for the race to **start**.

What time does the play **start**?

story

A **story** is a tale.
We tell **stories**.
We read **stories**, too.

Which **stories** are these?

sweep

Mary **sweeps** up leaves and litter.
She brushes them into a pile.

stay

To **stay** means to stop or wait.

The boy tells the dog to **stay**.
He tells him not to move.

swim

Mary can **swim**.
She uses her arms and legs to move through the water.

Do you like **swimming**?
Are you a **swimmer**?

t T

table
Tables are flat pieces of furniture with legs.

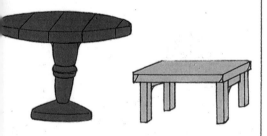

What are these **tables** for?

taste
When we eat things we **taste** them.

Sweets **taste** sweet.

Lemons **taste** sour.

television
A **television** brings pictures and sounds into our homes.

Television is called TV, too.

tail
These animals all have **tails**.

The kite has a **tail** too.

taxi
A **taxi** is a car that people pay to ride in.

ten
Ten tells us how many.

Here are **ten** tents.

tall
Tall means very high.

This tree is the **tallest**.

This tree is **taller**.

The tree is **tall**.

tea
Tea is a drink.

Tom pours **tea** from a **teapot**.

It is **teatime**.

tent

People sleep outdoors in **tents**.
People camp in **tents**.

telephone
A **telephone** carries sounds from one person to another.

With a **telephone** we can speak to people far away.

thick
The book is **thick**.
It has lots of pages.

Toms wears a **thick** jumper.
It keeps him warm.

thin
Thin means not wide or fat.

A sheet of paper is **thin**.

The man is **thin**.

ticket
A **ticket** is a piece of paper that shows we have paid.

You need **tickets** to travel on trains and buses.

together
Together means with someone or something

The children are all playing **together**.
The cat and dog are sitting **together**.

thirsty
When we have a **thirst** we want to drink.

Tom and Tim are **thirsty**.

tie
To **tie** means to join together.

Tim **ties** up the parcel.

Daddy wears a **tie** around his neck.

tongue
Your **tongue** helps you to taste.
Your **tongue** helps you to talk.

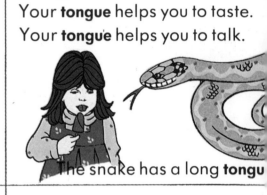

The snake has a long **tongue**.

three
Three tells us how many.

Here are **three** tigers.

time
Time tells us what part of the day it is.

Can you tell the **time**?

Clocks and watches tell us the **time**.

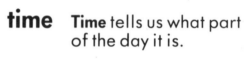
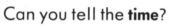
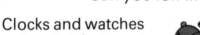

Eight o'clock. **Time** to get up.

Half past seven. **Time** to go to sleep.

What **time** is it now?

tool
Tools help make work easier.

spade

hammer

spanner

saw

hoe   rake

thumb
On each hand you have four fingers and a **thumb**.

Thumbs help us grip and lift things.

thunder
Thunder is a loud noise.

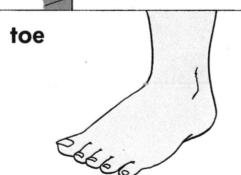

In storms we often hear **thunder** and see lightning.

toe

We have five **toes** on each foot.
Toes help us stand, walk and run.

tooth
Teeth help us talk and eat.

Tim has lost a **tooth**.

We clean our **teeth** with a **toothbrush** and **toothpaste**.

top
Top means high, or above.

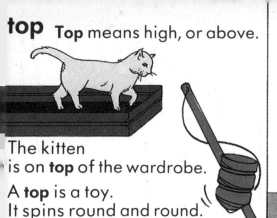

The kitten
is on **top** of the wardrobe.
A **top** is a toy.
It spins round and round.

touch
Touch means feel.

The girls' hands are **touching**.

Don't **touch** the pan. It's hot.

town
A **town** is a group of houses,
shops and offices.

A **town** is smaller than a city.
A **town** is bigger than a village.

toy
A **toy** is something to play with.
A **toy** rabbit isn't a real rabbit.

building bricks

teddy bear

marbles

bucket and spade

skipping rope   doll

train
A **train** carries people and goods.

The **train** is pulled by an engine.

Terry **trains** his dog.
He shows him what to do.

tree
A **tree** is a very big plant.

Do you know the names
of these **trees**?

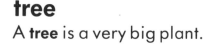

oak

ash

beech

fir   willow   chestnut

true
When something is **true**
it really happened.

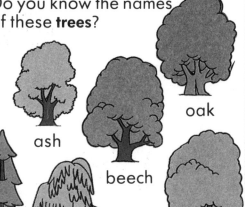

Is it **true** that you fell
in a puddle? Yes, it's **true**.

The boy is telling the **truth**.

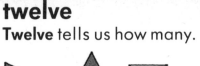

twelve

Twelve tells us how many.

Here are **twelve** triangles.
Dozen is another word for **twelve**.

twin
Twins are two children
born on the same day.

Twins have the same
Mummy and Daddy.

Some **twins** look alike.

two
Two tells us how many.

Here are **two** turtles.
And **two** tricycles.

typewriter
A **typewriter** is a writing machine.

A **typist** uses a **typewriter**.

tyre
Cars and bicycles run on **tyres**.

The car needs a new **tyre**.

The bicycle **tyre** needs more air.

u U

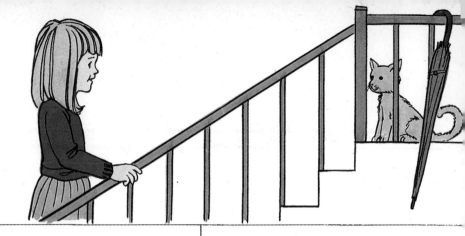

umbrella

An **umbrella** keeps off rain.
An **umbrella** keeps us dry.

underwear

Underwear are things we wear
under our outer clothes.

upstairs

Upstairs means
the top of the stairs.

Daddy is walking **upstairs**.
Spot is **upstairs** already.

under

Under means below, beneath.

The hat is **under** the chair.
The mouse is **under** the hat.

uniform

The children wear school **uniform**.
They wear the same clothes.

The policeman
wears a **uniform**, too.

use

Use means to do something with

Do you know how
to **use** a camera?
Mary has **used** one before.

underground

Underground means under
the ground.

Many things are **underground**.

up

Up means higher, above,
away from the ground.

The aeroplane flies **up**
into the sky.

String has many **uses**.
We can do lots of things with it.

understand

To **understand** is to know.

Mary **understands** the recipe.
She knows what it means.

upside-down

Upside-down means
turned the wrong way.

The boy is hanging **upside-down**.
The bucket is **upside-down**.

useful

Tools are **useful**.
They help us build things.

Books are **useful**.
They help us learn things.
Useful is anything that is of use.

v V

valley

A **valley** is the land between two hills.

The river runs along the **valley**.

value

Value means worth.
What is the **value** of the bike?

What is its price?
What is it worth?
Is the bike **valuable**?

van

A **van** is a kind of car used for carrying things.

FRED'S FLOWERS

What is this **van** carrying?

vase

A **vase** is made to hold flowers.

vegetable

Vegetables are parts of plants we eat as food.

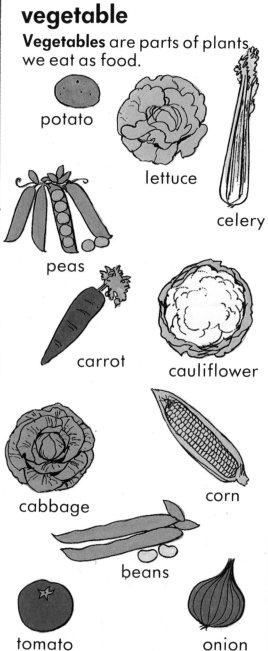

potato

lettuce

celery

peas

carrot

cauliflower

corn

cabbage

beans

tomato

onion

village

A **village** is a small town.

violin

Violins make music.

A **violin** has four strings.
It is played with a bow.

visit

Visit means to go and see.

Do you **visit** your grandparents?

Do you **visit** the library?

voice

When we speak we use our **voices**.

When we sing we use our **voices**.
Our **voice** is the noise we make.

volcano

A **volcano** is a mountain with a hole in the top.

Melted rock and steam pour from some **volcanoes**.

w W

wait

To **wait** means to stay.
I've forgotten my books.
Will you **wait** for me?

Yes, but hurry,
I'm not **waiting** long.

walk

To **walk** is to move on foot.

The people are all **walking**.
Wayne takes his dog for a **walk**.

wall

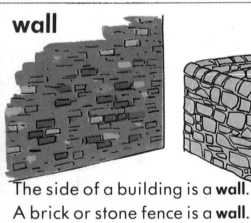

The side of a building is a **wall**.
A brick or stone fence is a **wall**.

wash

When we **wash** things we clean them.

Wendy **washes** her hands.
What is Daddy **washing**

watch

Watch means look.

William **watches** television.

What is the cat **watching**?

A **watch** tells the time.

water

Water is liquid.
Water is rain.
We drink **water**.
Plants drink **water**.

Water is in ponds,
rivers and the sea.

weather

Weather is how wet,
dry, hot or cold it is outside.

What kind of **weather**
are you having today?

windy   sunny

snowy   rainy

What kind of **weather**
do you like best?

week

A **week** is seven days.

There are 52 **weeks** in a year.

Do you know the days of the **week**

Monday
Tuesday
Wednesday
Thursday
Friday
Saturday
Sunday

Weekend means
Saturday and Sunday.

weigh

Weigh means find out how heavy something is.

The boy is being **weighed**.

The man **weighs** some sweets.

wet

Wet means covered with water.

When it rains
it is a **wet** day.
Mummy hangs out
the **wet** washing.

whale

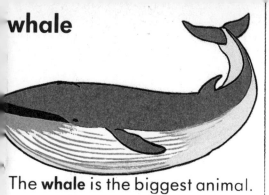

The **whale** is the biggest animal.
Whales live in the sea.

whole

Whole means all.
The boy ate a **whole** apple.

work
Work **is something to do.**

Work is a job.
Mummy **works** in the garden.
What **work** are these people doing?

wheel
Wheels are round.

Wheels help things move.
Mummy **wheels** the pram.

win
To **win** means to come first.

William **wins** the race.
He is the **winner**.

window
Windows let in air and light.
Wendy waves from her **window**.

world

Our **world** is the place we live in.
Our earth and sky is our **world**.

whisper
Whisper means speak very quietly.
Wendy is **whispering**.

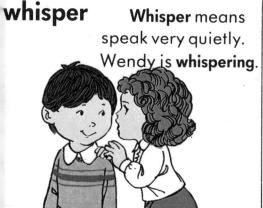

wing
Wings help things fly.

write
When we **write** we put words on paper.

Jane is **writing** her name.
Peter is **writing** his address.

white
White is a colour.

How many **white** things can you see?

woman
A **woman** is a grown-up.

Mummy is a **woman**.
Susie is a girl.
She will grow up to be a **woman**.

wrong
Wrong means not correct.
David got his sum **wrong**.

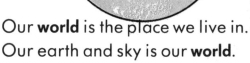

Wrong means not good, not right.
It is **wrong** to tell lies.

x X

Xmas
Xmas is another way of writing Christmas.

x-ray
X-rays take pictures of the insides of our bodies.

The doctor **x-rayed** Paul's arm to see if it was broken.

xylophone

A **xylophone** makes music.

y Y

yacht
A **yacht** is a small boat with sails.

yawn
We **yawn** when we feel sleepy.

We open our mouths wide and take a big breath.

year
A **year** is a measure of time.

There are 12 months in a **year**.

There are 365 days in a **year**, but 366 in a special leap **year**.

What **year** were you born?
What **year** is it now?

yell
A **yell** is a loud shout.

yellow
Yellow is a colour.

All these things are **yellow**.

yes

When we say **yes** we agree.
Will you come to my party? **Yes**!

yesterday
Yesterday is the day before today.

If today is Tuesday, **yesterday** was Monday.

z Z

yolk

The **yolk** is the yellow part of an egg.

zebra

A **zebra** is a striped animal.

It is like a small horse.

zoo

A **zoo** is a place where wild animals and birds are kept.

rhinoceros

chimpanzee

young

Young means not grown up.

A puppy is a **young** dog.
A **young** cat is a kitten.

zero

Zero tells us how many.

Zero means none at all.

tiger

toucan

your

Anything that is **yours** belongs to you.

Touch **your** head.
Clap **your** hands.

zigzag

Zigzag means to move from side to side.

The path **zigzags** through the park.

penguin

llama

yo-yo

A **yo-yo** is a toy.

zip

A **zip** fastens things together.

Zoe **zips** up her anorak.

antelope

sea lion

elephant